FINISHING YOUR ASSIGNMENT IN LIFE

Wale Babatunde

foreword by Dr. David Shibley

Christian Heritage Publication
An Imprint of
Great Commission Incorporation
25-27 Ruby Street
Off Old Kent Road
London
SE15 1LR
United Kingdom

ISBN: 978-0-9570933-4-8
Cover design: CCD Media Ltd
Book Transformation Work (Copy Editing & Proofreading) – Mrs. Nana Fosua Babatunde
Printed and bound in the UK.

Contents

Endorsements

"It was the sage King Solomon who said "a desire accomplished is sweet to the soul..." (Proverbs 13:19). There are only a few things more embarrassing than unfinished projects. The sad reality is that too many people live and die without fulfilling their life's assignment. This book is written to guide and motivate you to not only discover your life's purpose but more importantly to fulfil it and do so well."

Dr. Frank Ofosu-Appiah
Founder / Senior Pastor
All Nations Church
Atlanta, Georgia

"It is often said "The mystery of human existence lies not in just staying alive, but in finding something to live for". In other words, every man is created for a purpose and to solve a problem. Every man has a responsibility not only to discover their purpose in life but to pursue it and fulfil it as God ordained.

A wise man once said "the graveyard is the richest place on earth because it is here that you will find all the hopes and dreams that were never fulfilled, the books that were never written, the songs that were never sung, the inventions that were never shared, the cures that were never discovered, all because someone was too afraid to take that first step, keep with the problem, or determined to carry out their dream." (Les Brown)

This book is a complete 'guide' and 'reference manual'; a must-read for those who seek to make impact with their lives, finish their God-ordained assignments and leave a legacy of hope and strength to the next generation.

The insights contained in this book are informative, directional and life transforming. Everyone should aspire to read through at least once a year and refer to it as often as possible.

Rev. Wale Babatunde, I salute you for your passion and commitment to serve this generation and beyond, and for the invaluable wisdom contained in this book. I am confident that significant value has been added to humanity as a result of this work."

Michael Olawore
Senior Pastor
New Wine Church
London

Dedication

This book is dedicated to the triune God, who has given me the special privilege of witnessing fifty years, thirty of which I have preached The Gospel of Jesus Christ around the world. It has indeed been a great honour.

I also dedicate this book to all believers around the world, who are not just content with serving God but are doing everything to ensure they complete their assignment in life.

Acknowledgements

As the building of a nation cannot be achieved by one man overnight, so also could the production of this book never have been possible without the efforts, contributions, and inspiration of several others.

My special gratitude goes to my Church family who has stood by me over the years and given me the support and platform to fulfil my call. I further acknowledge my immediate family: Joshua, Grace, Jeremiah, and God's special gift to me, Nana Fosua. To my parents and siblings, I owe you a lot and to my personal assistant, Kolawole Sekoni, I appreciate you for your labour of love. To every mentor and ministerial colleague that has blessed me over the decades, I am beyond grateful and wish to say a very big 'Thank you'.

May we all finish our assignments in life!

Foreword

"Reading this important book can become a pivotal point for your future, and your lasting influence. Rev. Babatunde calls us to a life given to what matters most. He reminds us that a truly successful life is measured not by its duration but by its direction; not by its parties but by its purpose; not by what is amassed but by what is dispersed; not by the embracing of things but by embracing the One Thing – to love Jesus supremely and make Him loved by people everywhere."

Dr. David Shibley
Founder / World Representative
Global Advance
Dallas, Texas

INTRODUCTION

"And say to Archippus, 'Take heed to the ministry which thou hast received in the Lord, that thou fulfil it.'"
– Colossians 4:17 (KJV)

"Tell Archippus: "See to it that you complete the ministry you have received in the Lord."
– Colossians 4:17 (NIV)

Over the last few decades, there have been ample teachings – both on Christian and secular platforms, on subjects like 'Discovering and Harnessing your Potential and Destiny.' We have been taught that each one of us is unique and must therefore discover what we are best at and give our energies to it. We have also been greatly enlightened to believe that it is not enough to discover our potential and destiny, but we must do everything possible to develop ourselves so that we don't end up mediocre. In as much as these may be true, there is however a paucity of materials and teachings on the importance of completing one's assignment in life.

Some years ago, I sat under the teaching ministry of a respected Minister of The Gospel as he shared an opinion that a friend had shared with him. His friend expressed his belief that 95% of those called by God would never fulfil their assignments in their lifetime. This meant only about 5% would fulfil their destiny. This thought not only challenged me but it left an impression and determination in my heart to be among the 5% that will finish their race.

It is for this very reason that I have written this book to challenge you, the reader, not to just discover your God-given purpose, but to run your race and complete it in such a manner that will leave your footprints and legacy behind to the point where they cannot be erased for many generations to come.

In fulfilling your assignment, you must understand what it means to be successful from God's perspective. You must also guard against Satan's strategic wiles to derail you, which I call 'weapons of mass distraction!'

To finish your God-given assignment, you must also grasp the fact that life is governed or operates by seasons and like the sons of Issachar, you must know what to do in each season of your life.

As you pass through this life, you must not only live daily in the consciousness of your assignment but you must take Paul's counsel to Archippus as your watchword: "See to it that you complete the ministry you have received in the Lord." – Colossians 4:17 (NIV)

CHAPTER 1
THE GOD OF GENERATIONS

The God of the Bible is the God of Generations. I believe that God not only deals with individuals, families, churches and nations but also with generations.

I am convinced that God has specific assignments and purposes to be accomplished in every generation and therefore assigns specific individuals to achieve them.

> *"The book of the generation of Jesus Christ, the son of David, the son of Abraham. Abraham begat Isaac; and Isaac begat Jacob; and Jacob begat Judah and his brethren; And Judah begat Phares and Zara of Thamar; and Phares begat Esrom; and Esrom begat Aram; And Aram begat Aminadab; and Aminadab begat Naasson; and Naasson begat Salmon; And Salmon begat Booz of Rahab; and Booz begat Obed of Ruth; and*

Obed begat Jesse; And Jesse begat David the king; and David the king begat Solomon of her that had been the wife of Urias; And Solomon begat Roboam; and Roboam begat Abia; and Abia begat Asa; And Asa begat Josaphat; and Josaphat begat Joram; and Joram begat Ozias; And Ozias begat Joatham; and Joatham begat Achaz; and Achaz begat Ezekias; And Ezekias begat Manasses; and Manasses begat Amon; and Amon begat Josias; And Josias begat Jechonias and his brethren, about the time they were carried away to Babylon: And after they were brought to Babylon, Jechonias begat Salathiel; and Salathiel begat Zorobabel; And Zorobabel begat Abiud; and Abiud begat Eliakim; and Eliakim begat Azor; And Azor begat Sadoc; and Sadoc begat Achim; and Achim begat Eliud; And Eliud begat Eleazar; and Eleazar begat Matthan; and Matthan begat Jacob; And Jacob begat Joseph the husband of Mary, of whom was born Jesus, who is called Christ. So all the generations from Abraham to David are fourteen generations; and from David until the carrying away into Babylon are fourteen generations; and from the carrying away into Babylon unto Christ are fourteen generations."

- Matthew 1:1-17 (KJV)

The above passage has never been one of my favourites. If you are like me, anytime I am reading this chapter, I either skip these verses or try to read them very fast. Recently, I believe the Holy Spirit asked me a question – 'why did God bother to give us the names of every individual in Jesus' genealogy, starting from Abraham, the Jewish patriarch?'

Matthew the Gospeller, not only wanted to prove that Jesus was the King of the Jews by tracing His lineage to two important Jewish personalities: Abraham – the Jewish patriarch, and David – Israel's ideal king, but also to point out the place in history and God's divine agenda for each individual.

As I reflect on the Bible as a whole, I see generations: Adam the first man – came to fulfil God's divine purpose; Noah, another important personality, who not only was a preacher of righteousness but was also used by God to begin another phase in God's dealings with mankind after the deluge. And there was Abraham: He came to begin the Jewish race, a people that God would call His own. Moses, on the other hand, was raised by God as a deliverer – to bring his covenant people out of a land of slavery. Joseph had a unique place in God's scheme of things; even though most of his story seems gloomy, his life was yet so pivotal in helping to fulfil God's agenda in taking Israel into Egypt (their eventual land of bondage) and sustaining them during the famine.

As I also reflect on church history and some of the individuals that have shaped it, I cannot but agree that not only is our God a God of Generations but He also assigns each individual to a particular generation with a unique assignment.

John Wesley can be rightly described as a child born in due season; no doubt he couldn't have come at a better time. The moral and spiritual decadence of the 18th century called for a revivalist like him.

What about the 19th Century?

William Booth was a man of his generation. It was this saint, and the 'Salvation Army' he founded, that championed the cause of the poor, first in the east end of London, then across Britain and thereafter to several nations of the world.

We can go on and on. Every individual has a place in history! We have been placed by God in a particular generation for a unique assignment. Like Paul, we must be able to declare that we are children born in due time.

> *"And last of all he was seen of me also, as of one born out of due time."*
>
> - 1 Corinthians 15.8 (KJV)

Again like Esther, we must hold a sense of destiny for our generation.

> *"...and who knoweth whether thou art come to the kingdom for such a time as this?"*
>
> - Esther 4:14b (KJV)

CHAPTER 2
THE SMARTEST QUESTION

He was, and is probably still one of the greatest men that ever lived. He impacted his generation like no other. Even though he was a man of short stature, he stood taller than all his contemporaries. His life and writings have inspired and impacted millions in the last two millennia. He was born into nobility and sat under the best brains in his days. His zeal for religion was unparalleled until he met the true and risen Lord on his way to Damascus, armed with letters to go and arrest and persecute any 'of this way'. This true legend is Paul of Tarsus.

It was this very encounter that permanently altered his life causing him whilst giving his valedictory speech to the Ephesian elders, to declare unequivocally that no fear of affliction or death moved or concerned him, except one thing – to finish his course with joy, and the ministry which he had received from the Lord

Jesus Christ (Acts 20:24). Again at the end of his life, he was able to declare boldly that he had completed his assignment in life.

> *"I have fought a good fight, I have finished my course, I have kept the faith"*
>
> - 2 Timothy 4:7 (KJV)

The big question to ask then is 'what set this man that started on the wrong footing onto the right path, such that he could confidently state that he had completed his life's mission?'

I believe it was because he asked life's smartest question from the Only One who really mattered when it comes to the fulfilment of destiny: GOD. His question to the Lord during his encounter with him on his way to Damascus was "what will you have me do?"

> *"And he trembling and astonished said, Lord, what wilt thou have me to do?..."*
>
> - Acts 9:6a (KJV)

I believe that Paul was one of the smartest men that ever lived because he asked the smartest question that any right thinking person should ask. Why was his question the smartest question? You may ask.

First, he understood that God had a blueprint for everyone's life. Since He is the script writer and producer of life's drama, it behoves us to ask him this million dollar question.

> *"For I know the plans I have for you," declares the Lord, "plans to prosper you and not to harm you, plans to give you hope and a future."*
> - Jeremiah 29:11 (NIV)

This passage affirms as expressed above that God has a plan for all his children.

Secondly, not to ask God about our life's mission and assignment will amount to a wasted life. Once God is taken out of life's equation, the only option is to think up something of this earthly world and pursue it. This was what Paul did prior to his Damascus experience. The unfortunate part of it all is that many who are religious presume they are serving God. This is exactly the mind-set or theology of the Islamic terrorist and suicide bombers.

Thirdly, this smart question is the only antidote against the unnecessary competition that pervades Christendom today. Many people are busy today running other men's races because they have never taken out time to enquire from God what their life's assignment is.

Finally, I believe this was the smartest question because, ultimately, we are all going to be accountable to God on the day of judgement – we shall give an accurate account of our life and stewardship on earth.

"So we make it our goal to please him, whether we are at home in the body or away from it. For we must all appear before the judgment seat of Christ, so that each of us may receive what is due us for the things done while in the body, whether good or bad."

- 2 Corinthians 5:9-10 (NIV)

May God help us to ask the right question from Our Maker before it is too late!

CHAPTER 3
YOU ARE ON ASSIGNMENT

You are on a mission! You are on a divine mandate from the highest potentate. Perhaps, this is the greatest truth that I will like to pass on to you throughout this book.

The script for your life was written without any ambiguity before you were born. It was actually detailed in His Majesty's books before the foundations of the earth.

To Prophet Jeremiah, God declared that not only did He foreknow him, but his assignment here on earth had already been clearly set out.

> *"Then the word of the Lord came unto me, saying, Before I formed thee in the belly I knew thee; and before thou camest forth out of the womb I sanctified thee, and I ordained thee a prophet unto the nations."*
>
> - Jeremiah 1:4-5 (KJV)

Did you notice that before Jeremiah was born, God had already determined that he would be a prophet unto the nations? His assignment and destiny was to be a prophet, and his scope was the nations. For Jeremiah to have been involved in something else would have been folly, and a waste of his precious life.

You must understand that just as God had a life plan for Jeremiah, so has He for everyone. God's goal is for us to live according to His predetermined plan and allow Him work His good pleasures in and through us.

The greatest discovery anyone can make is not to discover gold in Ghana or oil in the fields of Kuwait or Saudi Arabia but to discover what has been written in the volumes of the books and pursue it. Until you discover and vigorously pursue your assignment, you are not living, but merely existing. I am grateful that I discovered my assignment early in life. By the special grace of God, I have been pursuing my divine assignment for three decades. One thing is clear when you are living out your assignment: you will experience a fulfilment, joy and peace that nothing else can offer you – not even millions of dollars, pounds or euros.

I can recollect very vividly, after my university education, my father got me a job in one of the parastatals in Nigeria. The income was not bad, and according to him, it gave me some stability. It was a very commendable gesture from a father who wanted his son to succeed at all costs. However, for the three months I worked at this government organization, I was a frustrated young man. Soon after I assumed duty, I felt demoralised, lost my peace, and just wanted to leave. After enduring this 'torture' for three precious months of my life, I resigned, and to date, I have only worked for one employer - who happens to be God Himself! My assignment in life, from the onset of my call, has been very clear – to bring men and women to the saving knowledge of Jesus Christ, to challenge the church in taking the whole Gospel to the whole world, and to be a clear prophetic voice – speaking to governments and nations!

JESUS – A MAN ON ASSIGNMENT
Jesus, not only came to this world as God's perfect lamb and sacrifice for our sins, but He came also to show us how to live as Sons and Daughters of God. The scriptures declare that Jesus came to do and live what was written about Him prior to his incarnation.

> *"Then said I, Lo, I come (in the volume of the book it is written of me,) to do thy will, O God."*
> - Hebrews 10:7 (KJV)

> *"Then said I, Lo, I come: in the volume of the book it is written of me, I delight to do thy will, O my God: yea, thy law is within my heart."*
> - Psalm 40:7-8 (KJV)

27

Throughout the Gospel, we see Jesus repeatedly declare that He was a sent one and His delight was to do the will of Him that sent Him!

"Jesus saith unto them, My meat is to do the will of him that sent me, and to finish his work."
- John 4:34 (KJV)

"For I came down from heaven, not to do mine own will, but the will of him that sent me."
- John 6:38 (KJV)

May Jesus' prayer, passion and experience also be ours!

YOU ARE A SENT ONE

Whether you know it or not, you have been sent. There are too many Christians who are waiting for man's recognition, affirmation or titles before they carry out their life's assignment. This is totally wrong! While I believe that accolades and recognition have their place in life, the desire for them should never stand in one's way of carrying out their purpose.

Jesus declared to His first disciples, and by extension to us that, just as He was sent as a missionary among the Godhead, so also have we been sent.

"Then said Jesus to them again, Peace be unto you: as my Father hath sent me, even so send I you."
- John 20:21 (KJV)

"As thou hast sent me into the world, even so have I also sent them into the world."

- John 17:18 (KJV)

WHAT IS MY ASSIGNMENT?

For most of you reading this book, you might have discovered your assignment in life and are faithfully and strongly pursuing them. However, there are some reading, who are asking the question – 'what is my assignment; what am I supposed to be doing?' To these precious ones, my response is:

1. **To Fulfil The Great Commission** - Did you notice that I said the Great Commission and not the great omission? Several Christians are unnecessarily busy with many things to the point where they have missed or omitted the most important assignment given to the Church by our Saviour. This marching order, he gave after His resurrection, declaring:

   "And Jesus came and spake unto them, saying, All power is given unto me in heaven and in earth. Go ye therefore, and teach all nations, baptizing them in the name of the Father, and of the Son, and of the Holy Ghost"

   - Matthew 28:18-19 (KJV)

   Again,

   "And he said unto them, Go ye into all the

29

world, and preach the gospel to every creature"
— Mark 16:15 (KJV)

As Christians, we have been called and commissioned to take the Gospel to the whole world – from Jerusalem to the ends of the world. (Acts 1:8)

2. **To Be A Change Agent** – Following the above, we have also been charged with the vocation of being the change and preservation agents in our societies. Wherever we find ourselves, we are to be, not only the difference makers, but the preserving factor that stops our towns, cities, and nations from destruction.

"Ye are the salt of the earth... Ye are the light of the world..."
— Matthew 5:13a, 14a (KJV)

3. **Called For A Specific Assignment** – Apart from the Great Commission and carrying out our vocation as salt and light in a decadent and degenerating generation, each one of us has been called and commissioned by God for a unique assignment. I always say that no two pastors, evangelists, apostles, prophets or teachers are the same. Our personalities are unique and so also are our respective purposes in life. Take a look at Paul and Peter, both of whom were great servants of God in their own rights, but their assignments were totally different. The first was

commissioned as an Apostle to the Gentiles, while the latter's mission and ministry were mainly to the Jews. Each one of us has a unique place and role, just as the members of our bodies. As such, it is not only our responsibility to discover our assignments, but we are also to carry them out with the utmost speed, diligence and precision, for the King's business demands urgency.

CHAPTER 4

YOUR ULTIMATE GOAL IN LIFE

"However, I consider my life worth nothing to me; my only aim is to finish the race and complete the task the Lord Jesus has given me—the task of testifying to the good news of God's grace."

- Acts 20:24 (NIV)

In life, there are many goals that most of us will set. From the time you are able to reason and take responsibility for your life, you will likely set goals. For example, at different times, a student will want to set educational goals: to excel in primary, secondary, and tertiary institutions. Many will also have financial goals: to get out of debt or to save the first million. Other people will set goals to get married at a certain age, build or buy their home debt-free, build a five thousand seating capacity church, or win an Olympic gold medal.

Paul the erudite Apostle, however, had what I call the ultimate goal in life. He had an overriding passion! It was to finish his race. Paul knew that what mattered before God and in eternity was that we finished our race in life. This goal seemed to consume Paul. Read the Pauline epistles and you cannot but feel the pulse of a man who was determined to finish his race at all costs. The legal luminary declared to the Ephesian elders what his life's ambition was – to finish his race!

Towards the end of Paul's life, he now reviews his life and ministry. How did he score himself? Let's hear from the horse's mouth:

> *"For I am now ready to be offered, and the time of my departure is at hand. I have fought a good fight, I have finished my course, I have kept the faith"*
>
> - 2 Timothy 4:6-7 (KJV)

This is what I call the ultimate success. He declared on authority that 'I have fought a good fight, I have finished my course, I have kept the faith.' Most people in life today don't even understand that there's a divine assignment that has been allotted them, how much more finishing it.

I believe that among the life goals of many is the desire to come out of the university with a first class, buy the latest car or even complete a building project.

As good and lofty as all these may be, they will likely not have an eternal significance.

What must consume our hearts is to finish the assignment that God has given to us. We must endeavour to complete every task, assignment, dream, and vision that God has placed before us! This is what should keep our focus on the finishing line! This is where our energies should be directed or expended.

May I suggest that everything that has to do with the salvation of souls: turning sinners from darkness to light (from the power of Satan to the power of God), should be number one on our agenda. This should be our utmost priority.

Paul's ultimate goal, according to him, was to "... testify to the good news of God's grace" – Acts 20:24b (NIV). Nothing is more important! Nothing is loftier. This is one thing that makes angels and the whole of heaven celebrate.

Is soul winning, depopulating hell and extending the frontiers of the kingdom of heaven your ultimate goal in life? If your answer is in the negative, you need to make it your ultimate goal this instant!

CHAPTER 5

THE DIFFERENT SEASONS OF LIFE
(Ecclesiastes 3:1-8)

"To every thing there is a season, and a time to every purpose under the heaven"
                                            - Ecclesiastes 3:1 (KJV)

"While the earth remaineth, seedtime and harvest, and cold and heat, and summer and winter, and day and night shall not cease."
                                            - Genesis 8:22 (KJV)

From the very beginning of creation, God established an order – life was to operate by seasons. For example, in the temperate regions, we have four seasons – spring, summer, autumn and winter. Each of these seasons comes with their peculiar characteristics: having distinctive opportunities and challenges. An understanding of these seasons and their peculiarities makes us respond appropriately, otherwise, we stand to lose.

I will like to make a few observations. Firstly, just as we have differed seasons in the natural, so also are there corresponding seasons in the spiritual. Secondly, understanding of the various seasons of life will help us do the right thing in each season. We will thus be like the sons of Issachar, who had an understanding of the times, and knew what Israel ought to do.

> *"And of the children of Issachar, which were men that had understanding of the times, to know what Israel ought to do..."*
> - 1 Chronicles 12:32a (KJV)

Every one of us must understand that we have been placed on earth for a period or life span. Moses, the Man of God, declared this life span to be 70 or 80, even though many will not live up till this age.

> *"Our days may come to seventy years, or eighty, if our strength endures; yet the best of them are but trouble and sorrow, for they quickly pass, and we fly away."*
> - Psalm 90:10 (NIV)

Within our life span, that is especially those who live up till seventy or eighty, we experience or go through seasons. Every year, at least in the temperate regions, we go through four seasons:

1. Spring – This is characterised by plants budding and becoming green.
2. Summer – The season of harvest. It is the season when things are bright.
3. Autumn/Fall – The temperate cools again; leaves begin to fall.
4. Winter – The weather becomes extremely harsh and dark with all the leaves from the trees fallen.

Just as the natural order of things has their peculiar characteristics, so also are the various seasons of our lives. In as much as this may not cut across to all, it applies to the majority. Dr Sola Fola-Alade, a well-respected Christian leader, has written a beautiful piece on the four seasons of life in his book "Discover Your Hidden Treasures" (Vision media communications, London 2002. Pages 105-113.)

1. **Spring (0 - 25) years** – The Season of Foresight. This is the period of your life when you bud. It is the season of growth; a time to prepare, plan and learn. It is the season of seedtime. It is the time to lay proper and strong foundations for the years to come. It is important to note that whatever seeds you sow during this season, good or bad, will affect you for the rest of your life.

A critical phenomenon during this season is your educational development. Have you noticed that for most people, age 0 – 25 is when they lay their educational foundation. By the age of 25, many would have graduated from university. The education they acquire, or the lack of it, is bound to affect their productivity and fulfilment of life's assignment. By the age of 25, I had already graduated from the university, and the education that I acquired has contributed immensely in the fulfilment of my life's purpose.

Also, during this season, you would have made occupational and career choices. By the age of 25, most individuals would have been set in the path of their career or occupation.

2. **Summer (25 – 50) years** – Season of Insight. This is the harvest season of your life. It is the time of your life when you begin to reap the fruits of your spring season. It is at this time that you mature in your career, profession or calling. For example, most Ministers of the Gospel that I know, who excelled, would have or almost reached their peak during this season. This season also is the time of maturity, stability, and the accumulation of wealth and resources.

The summer of your life is also the time you raise children. For a very high percentage of people, at the end of your summer years, most of your children would have almost completed their education. Can you imagine someone at the peak of their summer season, just beginning to take their primary or secondary education seriously?

3. **Autumn (50 – 75) years** – Hindsight. This is the season in one's life when you begin to wind down, leading to retirement. It is a period of passing down the wisdom and experience acquired over the years. At this time, you begin to discover that time is closing in on you because you don't have too much of it ahead of you to fulfil the dreams that you once cherished. This is when people encounter the mid-life crisis! Can you imagine someone in their autumn season trying to pursue what they should have accomplished in their spring season? This is why a lot of people have regrets when they grow old; because they have wasted their youth.

If you are a young person reading this book, I beg of you not to waste your life by investing your time, energies and other resources in unprofitable, ungodly and un-commanded ventures.

4. **Winter (75 and above) years** – Our winter season is the period of transition from Mortality to Immortality. It is the season to exit the world. Unfortunately, most people never prepare for this season. I have met folks who are in their eighties and are not even prepared to die. The prophet's word to King Hezekiah should be a good counsel to everyone

in this season – 'Set your house in order because you are going to die.'

> *"In those days was Hezekiah sick unto death. And Isaiah the prophet the son of Amoz came unto him, and said unto him, Thus saith the Lord, Set thine house in order: for thou shalt die, and not live."*
>
> - Isaiah 38:1 (KJV)

This is the season of succession. When, like King David, you begin to hand over notes to your successor. Nothing is more foolish than to depart this world, after you have accomplished a lot, without raising a successor. Remember, there's no success without a successor. One of the key things in living a fulfilled life is to hand over the baton to the next generation. Moses handed over to Joshua; Elijah to Elisha; Paul to Timothy, Titus and many others; Jesus to the twelve, and then to the seventy disciples.

So many individuals in different fields of endeavour accomplish great feats, but never invest in or raise the next generation.

May God help us to be like the sons of Issachar, who were men of understanding of the times, and knew what Israel ought to do!

CHAPTER 6
REDEEMING THE TIME

"See then that ye walk circumspectly, not as fools, but as wise, Redeeming the time, because the days are evil"

- Ephesians 5:15-16 (KJV)

I am totally convinced that we are in the very last minutes of the last days! I believe with all of my heart that God is wrapping up everything on earth. We are racing towards the climax of the ages. I believe that my generation will witness the rapture of the church – if not, certainly that of my children.

We are now on a countdown to the Bridegroom coming to take His bride. Time is not on our side. The church has wasted so much time and energy on unprofitable ventures and projects.

As I write, my eyes are filled with tears about the

opportunities that I have wasted. As I reflect on my life, my heart is totally broken at the way I have wasted my life doing things that do not have eternal value. I regret not putting my best to the work that has been committed into my hands.

I have written this chapter particularly for the younger generation – who probably still have more years ahead of them. Please don't waste your youth. Please don't expend your energies on things that will not count for eternity.

Every activity, project, energy exacted and time spent will be weighed in terms of eternal significance and whether or not it is a commanded work. You must endeavour to buy back or redeem wasted time – time that has been expended on unprofitable ventures and unfruitful works of darkness.

In order to redeem our time, we need divine wisdom! Wisdom will help you distinguish between things that are necessary and important and those which are irrelevant and unfruitful. We need wisdom and discernment not to waste our time.

Some of you reading this book will have to spend less time sleeping; many others will cut short their leisure; while some will have to do away with relationships that are a waste of time. Time wasters are destiny destroyers!

To redeem your time, you must learn to say "no" to certain people without feeling guilty, because your time is your life!

CHAPTER 7
ONLY ONE LIFE!

I want to share with you something that is a fact but most humans never really give deep thought to. This thought, not only often brings back tonnes of regrets and tears at times for opportunities that I have wasted, but also inspires me to want to give my very best in all I do now for the remaining part of my sojourn on earth.

God indeed is said to be a God of second chances. He is a God of grace, love and mercy. There are many things in life that you can be afforded a second chance to redeem your mistakes. For example, in most educational institutions, when you fail or perform below standard, you can be given the opportunity to retake the exam or the class.

Many people don't do too well or make a shipwreck of their relationships or marriages, but can experience a blissful second or even third marriage. I have heard of friends and families who attempted their driving tests about ten times before they finally passed. There are many things that I have had to repeat more than once before I finally got them. I am sure you probably have had similar experiences.

In as much as the above may be true, we however have only one opportunity to live this life. Have you ever heard the saying -"Life has no duplicate"? In other words, once it ends, that is it. We will never have the opportunity to live on earth twice. No one will have the opportunity of going through the four seasons of life – spring, summer, autumn and winter, twice. Once you have gone through any or all of these seasons, it cannot be repeated. I will never regain my teenage years; they're gone forever. It doesn't matter how hard I pray, they're gone. Sometimes, I wish someone taught me what I know now. I wish I didn't waste any of the opportunities that God presented me when I was a lot younger.

> *"And as it is appointed unto men once to die, but after this the judgment"*
> - Hebrews 9:27 (KJV)

Friend, you will only have just one opportunity to live this life; God has only gifted you with this one life – to be 50, 60, 70, 80, or even 40 years. Within your life span, you are expected by God, not only to discover your life's purpose, but to finish your race or assignment. This is why you must get serious. You must get going. Unlike in the game of football where you have the second half, in the game of life, there is only one session; once it expires, that is it. Again, unlike football which gives you ninety minutes to play, in the game of life, you don't have control over the number of days or years you will spend on earth. For some, they will spend 40 years, others will be given 60 years, and not many will reach 100 years before their lease expires.

If we all bear this truth always in our hearts, we will maximise our lives and pursue our assignments with vigour, purpose and precision. Once I understood that I will only tread this path of life once, my motto in life has been the wise counsel of King Solomon:

"Whatsoever thy hand findeth to do, do it with thy might; for there is no work, nor device, nor knowledge, nor wisdom, in the grave, whither thou goest"

- Ecclesiastes 9:10 (KJV)

Remember, once you have taken in your last breath and given up your ghost; once the final whistle has been blown by the giver of life, there's no going back on your deeds or actions. This is even what makes it scarier because death could be knocking at your door at any given moment. Also, Jesus can descend from heaven to rapture genuine believers, which will bring your works to an end.

47

Since we now understand that we will only have one opportunity in life, what manner of person should we each be? How should we live our lives?

My suggestion is – we must always:

1. Endeavour to do everything to give God glory. We don't have the luxury in our short life to glorify flesh or anything, other than God.
2. Do everything possible to invest our time, talents, and resources into eternal and not mundane things. By this, I mean things that will matter at the end of time.
3. Give soul winning our utmost priority. There are few things in eternity that will be as valuable and priceless as the souls of the redeemed.
4. Give our best while we are living.
5. Love and forgive more, keeping no record of wrong.
6. Spend quality time with the Holy Spirit and our loved ones – our family and the precious souls that God has destined for us to meet on the path of life.

CHAPTER 8
LEAVE YOUR FOOTPRINTS

"For we are his workmanship, created in Christ
Jesus unto good works, which God hath before
ordained that we should walk in them"
- Ephesians 2:10 (KJV)

You are a history maker! You were created by God, called and commissioned to make your mark here on earth. Every child of God is unique and therefore a star.

As I write, I am going through the hall of fame in the book of Hebrews, chapter 11, where the Holy Spirit singles out certain individuals, who not only left their mark on the sands of time but were men and women that pleased God - individuals such as Abel, Enoch, Noah, Abraham, Jacob, Joseph, Moses, Rahab, Gideon, Barak, Samson, David, Samuel, and many others. Why did the Holy Spirit pen their names and their feats or accomplishments? I believe that God wants us to be inspired by their lives.

Again, I often try to visualise how heaven will be like. Many Christians think that all that the Redeemed will be doing is to sing and worship God and the Lamb. I am convinced that there will be abundance of worship; however, there will be lots of other activities taking place. Heaven will be filled with fun, shocks and surprises. I believe we shall have the opportunity of meeting all the Old and New Testament Saints. I have often wondered what it will be like the day I meet with Abraham, Moses, Joshua, Elijah and Elisha, just to mention these few from the Old Testament, and what it will be like when they begin to recount their exploits for God – all these without the indwelling of the Holy Spirit!

What will it be like, the day we meet with Peter, who preached just a single sermon and three thousand people turned to the Lord? How shall we feel, when he begins to narrate his experience of walking on water? What will meeting Paul be like? – The Apostle who not only wrote seventy-five percent of the New Testament but did more than anyone in establishing the Apostolic Church!

I wonder how it will be when John Wesley begins to recount how dark and gloomy it was, and how God used him to change the tide of things, such that rather than experience a revolution like France, God visited England with a national revival that transformed the nation.

I look forward to meeting Evan Roberts - the famous Welsh revivalist, Charles Spurgeon – the most famous preacher in England during his day.

It will surely be an interesting encounter when we meet some of Britain's social reformers, who not only blessed and changed many lives but also left their footprints on the sands of time. They include - William Wilberforce, Lord Shaftesbury, Elizabeth Fry, John Howard, Florence Nightingale, and Mary Slessor, just to mention these few.

I look forward to meeting some of my heroes and hearing interesting stories of how they impacted their generation and made God famous. They include Apostle Joseph Ayo Babalola – The founder of the Christ Apostolic Church, and the man who was reputed to have ignited the first modern revival in the nation of Nigeria.

I can't wait to see David Livingstone, Oswald J. Smith, Prophet T. O. Obadare, Leonard Ravenhill – mission statesmen and revivalists who have inspired me more than anyone in the area of missions and evangelism. These were men who left their footprints on the sands of time.

The big question is – are you going to live and die as a "Nobody"? Are you going to deny your generation of what is birthed in the inside of you? Are you going to impact your generation and change the course of history, or be content with mediocrity?

The choice is yours!

CHAPTER 9
THINKING LEGACY

There are many things in my estimation which I believe will help inspire most people to vigorously pursue destiny and finish their life's assignment. However, one of the most potent forces is when we think legacy.

First, let me define the word Legacy. Legacy refers to something handed down from one generation to the next. It could also be a gift by will, especially money or other personal property. ("Legacy." *Merriam-Webster.com.* Merriam-Webster, 2016. Web. 26 October 2016)

By now, I am pretty sure you have made up your mind to not only finish your race in life, but to make your mark. Most people on earth live and die without giving deep consideration to the kind of legacy that they are going to leave behind. One way or the other, all of us are going to leave legacies behind – some very significant, others not so significant; some godly, while others ungodly and wicked.

Some legacies will be local, others regional, many national, while very few will be global. Several people's legacies will be limited to specific spheres like sports, music or religion, while others will cut across several spheres and generations. Whatever the case, you must make up your mind to leave a lasting, godly legacy that will be difficult to erase for many generations.

When you hear the following names, I'm sure you not only think legacy, but also that they were men and women who positively impacted their generations for the better

- Jesus
- The Wright brothers
- Madam Theresa
- Isaac Newton
- John Wesley
- Dr Billy Graham
- William Wilberforce
- David Livingstone
- William Carey
- Nelson Mandela
- Jesse Boot
- Michael Faraday

- Robert Boyle
- Lord Shaftesbury
- Dr Thomas Barnardo
- Mary Slessor
- William Booth

Conversely, if I mention the names – Hitler, Stalin, Idi-Amin, Osama-Bin-Laden, Jim Jones of the famous Guayana tragedy, what readily comes to mind is murder, pain and possibly agony.

SOME THINGS THAT PEOPLE LEAVE BEHIND

These are some of the common things parents leave behind for their wards after they have departed this world:

1. Money – The value of which depreciates with inflation especially in today's world.
2. Cars – The moment you drive a car out of a showroom, the value begins to depreciate.
3. Houses – As good and as desirable as houses are, I have discovered that every generation tends to come up with their own designs because of the evolving nature of taste/preference.

A look at most things parents leave behind as legacies will reveal one basic fact – most of them are limited to material prosperity. Material things are excellent and desirable, however, it must be said that prosperity that is only beneficial to its owner is not the kind of legacy that the world would remember you for. God's commission to Abraham is still true for us in the 21st century.

> *"And I will make of thee a great nation, and I will bless thee, and make thy name great, and thou shalt be a blessing."*
>
> - Genesis 12:2 (KJV)

The real purpose of God's blessing is for us to be channels or conduits of blessing. There are many things that I believe we can leave behind as legacies that far outweigh material things. One of such is a good name. The wise man – Solomon, declares unequivocally that a good name is far better than riches.

> *"A good name is rather to be chosen than great riches, and loving favour rather than silver and gold."*
>
> - Proverbs 22:1 (KJV)

The Bible is littered with several people that left a good legacy:

Dorcas (Acts 9:36-39) – The Bible describes her as a disciple in Joppa, who was full of good works and alms-deeds. Like all mortals, one day she was faced with a problem – sickness, which eventually led to her death.

Rather than bury her, the disciples in the city decided to lay her in the upper chamber, calling for the apostolic leader, Peter, to come and pray for her; I guess in order to raise her from the dead. It is interesting to note that the loss would have been too much for them to bear, as this godly saint put smiles on people's faces while she was alive. People showed tangible evidence of her legacy, for example, coats and garments she had made for the underprivileged. This is the kind of legacy that I am talking about: acts of kindness so powerful and impactful that people would even refuse to bury her.

Another person in the scriptures that left a lasting legacy was Mary – the person who anointed Jesus with precious ointment. For the good deed that she did, Jesus declared that wherever the Gospel was preached throughout the whole world, the story of this woman would be told. This is a pure legacy!

"Now when Jesus was in Bethany, in the house of Simon the leper, There came unto him a woman having an alabaster box of very precious ointment, and poured it on his head, as he sat at meat. But when his disciples saw it, they had indignation, saying, To what purpose is this waste? For this ointment might have been sold for much, and given to the poor. When Jesus understood it, he said unto them, Why trouble ye the woman? for she hath wrought a good work upon me. For ye have the poor always with you; but me ye have not always. For in that she hath poured this ointment on my body, she did it for my burial. Verily I say unto you, wheresoever this gospel shall be preached in the whole world, there shall also this, that this woman hath done, be told for a memorial of her."

- Matthew 26:6-13 (KJV)

So what are some of the things that we can do to leave an enduring legacy that will both count for time and eternity?

1. Investing in Soul Winning – Anything that will bring people to the saving knowledge of Jesus Christ.
2. Alleviating poverty in the society.
3. Education – investing in Christ-centred and God-honouring education.
4. Justice and Equality – standing for justice, particularly for the voiceless and downtrodden.
5. Healthcare – helping people with their health, in the name of the Lord.

The list is endless!

CHAPTER 10

FINISH YOUR RACE

"But none of these things move me, neither count I my life dear unto myself, so that I might finish my course with joy, and the ministry, which I have received of the Lord Jesus, to testify the gospel of the grace of God."

- Acts 20:24 (KJV)

"However, I consider my life worth nothing to me; my only aim is to finish the race and complete the task the Lord Jesus has given me—the task of testifying to the good news of God's grace."

- Acts 20:24 (NIV)

Dr Bobby Clinton, Professor of Leadership at Fuller Theological Seminary in Pasadena, California, did a comparative study of leadership in the scriptures. He published these findings in a book entitled *"The Mantle of a Mentor"*. His research showed, among many things that there are about one thousand leaders mentioned in the Bible. Of these, approximately one hundred are given prominent mention. Dr Clinton demonstrated that only about 30% of these leaders finished well; this means 2 out of 3 did not finish well. What a sobering thought!

Life is filled with incomplete projects, dreams and aspirations. If there's something that needs to be restored unto the church today, it is the finishing spirit! We need to understand the importance of finishing a project or race.

What is important is not the number of projects that we embark on but rather how many we finish at the end of the day. It is not how we begin in life but how we finish. Most people will not remember how you came into the world, but the majority will keep a mental log of how you exit!

As I write, the Olympic Games in Rio, Brazil is in full swing. Last night, I watched the women cyclists battle it out for several kilometres. The interesting thing about the race was that all the competing cyclists started the race, but not everyone finished it; some fell along the way due to one problem or the other. The painful thing is that most of these women had been practising for a number of years.

The Finishing Mind-set

One attitude we must all inculcate if we are going to finish our assignment in life is the finishing mind-set. What counts is not how we begin the race of life – your business, marriage, education or ministry; it is whether or not you finish it. If we all have this mind-set, it will make us focused and humble, and we will not celebrate prematurely.

Today, I see too many people celebrate too early in life. Can you imagine an athlete or a football club begins to celebrate when they are only halfway through the competition? As I look at so many people, including Ministers of the Gospel, we seem to receive too many accolades and celebrations as though the work is already done, when we have only just started our assignments.

After serving God in ministry for 30 years, I have never been more concerned than now about whether or not I will finish the race set before me by God. I am equally burdened with the thought of whether I will run the race according to the rules – lest after running, I am disqualified.

"Know ye not that they which run in a race run all, but one receiveth the prize? So run, that ye may obtain. And every man that striveth for the mastery is temperate in all things. Now they do it to obtain a corruptible crown; but we an incorruptible. I therefore so run, not as uncertainly; so fight I, not as

one that beateth the air: But I keep under my
body, and bring it into subjection: lest that by
any means, when I have preached to others, I
myself should be a castaway."

- 1 Corinthians 9:24-17 (KJV)

In my lifetime, I have seen many individuals, male and female, young and old, exit this world. I have also been to several funeral services and I have conducted a few. One question that always confronts me is – did this person finish their assignment? Did they exit knowing fully well that their job is done and there's nothing more to do or were they taken out before their time?

Nothing confronts the living more when grieving for a loved one than knowing that the deceased is a child of God, and thus their place is assured in heaven, but more importantly, that this person took serious their life's purpose, and they completed it.

If there's anything more that I'll desire, it is to finish my assignment. By the time I exit this world, I want to make sure that there's nothing left to be done from heaven's perspective.

JESUS' EXAMPLE

Jesus, our perfect example, was focused on one thing from the onset – to finish His assignment! He knew why He was on earth, and He would not let anything or anyone distract Him from running His race. Jesus once declared what His goal was:

"Jesus saith unto them, My meat is to do the will of him that sent me, and to finish his work."
- John 4:34 (KJV);

Again,

"But I have greater witness than that of John: for the works which the Father hath given me to finish..."
- John 5:36a (KJV)

One thing is clear from Jesus' words – He knew He had to finish His assignment.

In no other way are we certain that Jesus completed His earthly assignment than when He declared in the following words:

"I have glorified thee on the earth: I have finished the work which thou gavest me to do."
- John 17:4 (KJV)

Again on the cross, when His redemptive work and mission on earth had been completed, He declared unequivocally *"... It is finished..."* (John 19:30).

When a person finishes their assignment, it doesn't really matter how long they lived for. I have often asked folks of their preference – Long Life or Fulfilled Destiny? We live in a society or age that is so obsessed with long life. Everyone wants to live long. I have been to prayer meetings and conventions that were based on long life.

While this is desirable, the reality of it is that not everyone will die old like Abraham, Moses or Jacob. Many of God's choicest servants died in the prime of their lives – some in their twenties, others thirties and forties. I even once buried one of my beloved sons in the faith, who was barely eighteen years old.

Judging by our modern standards, Jesus died young – at the age of thirty-three. Should he have died today, it is almost certain that there will not be a dearth of sorrow and agony. However, the question we often overlook is - did He finish his assignment? Did He complete His work?

Ask yourself this: what else should a person be doing on earth if their work is done? Don't forget, what is so crucial is that we finish our race.

Receive Grace to finish your race!

CHAPTER 11
THE FINISHING CONSCIOUSNESS

"For as he thinketh in his heart, so is he..."
                                    - Proverbs 23:7a (KJV)

In this chapter, I will want to challenge you to begin to live in the consciousness of your assignment or life's purpose. Anyone that is going to finish their race in life must daily live in the consciousness of their assignment. The question that we must frequently ask ourselves is "Am I in God's program or agenda for my life? Is what I am doing at the moment part of my God-given assignment or simply an un-commanded work?"

Our actions in life are always fuelled by our thoughts. Our life therefore, is a summation of our thought life. We will always gravitate towards our predominant thought; as a result, if we cultivate a finishing consciousness, the likelihood is that we are better positioned to complete our assignment.

A person with a finishing consciousness will always want to align whatever they are doing with their purpose in life. Their resources, time, energies, relationships, programmes, etc. will all align to what they have been called to do.

JESUS is our perfect example. He never went anywhere except it was part of His assignment. No wonder He declared:

> *"...Very truly I tell you, the Son can do nothing by himself; he can do only what he sees his Father doing, because whatever the Father does the Son also does."*
>
> - John 5:19 (NIV)

Again He professed,

> *"I must work the works of him that sent me, while it is day: the night cometh, when no man can work."*
>
> - John 9:4 (KJV)

The above scriptures reveal something important – Jesus lived in the consciousness of His assignment. He was not going to do or embark on anything except it was sanctioned from above. He understood the importance of sticking to His assignment in life. Even when Jesus did something as mundane as attending a social gathering, He was still conscious of His purpose and mission in life.

At the marriage in Cana of Galilee, Jesus' statement and demeanour at a point revealed how conscious and particular he was about His assignment; He declared:

"... Woman, what have I to do with thee? mine hour is not yet come."

- John 2:4 (KJV).

In other words, He knew what he had to do at every given time and on every occasion.

PAUL, the learned apostle, also lived his life in the consciousness of finishing his assignment. This stayed with him from the beginning to the end.

Do you want to finish your race and hear the glorious affirmation – "Well done, thou good and faithful servant"? If your answer is in the affirmative, then, you need to begin to live your life daily in the consciousness of your life's mission.

CHAPTER 12
DOES GOD WANT YOU TO BE SUCCESSFUL?

"Only be thou strong and very courageous, that thou mayest observe to do according to all the law, which Moses my servant commanded thee: turn not from it to the right hand or to the left, that thou mayest prosper withersoever thou goest. This book of the law shall not depart out of thy mouth; but thou shalt meditate therein day and night, that thou mayest observe to do according to all that is written therein: for then thou shalt make thy way prosperous, and then thou shalt have good success."

- Joshua 1:7-8 (KJV)

"Beloved, I wish above all things that thou

mayest prosper and be in health, even as thy soul prospereth."

- 3 John 1:2 (KJV)

Does God want us to be successful? Is it God's will for every child of God to be successful? If so, what does it mean to be successful?

Over the last few decades, we have heard tonnes of teachings, both in the electronic and print media, on the subject of success! The church of the 21st century is therefore not short of success, prosperity and motivational teachers. Sadly enough, many are guilty of taking their teachings to the extreme!

WHAT DOES SUCCESS LOOK LIKE?

After having been a Christian for almost four decades and after having listened to several thousands of teachings and read many books, the question that occupies my mind is – *what does a successful Christian life look like?*

Can we be missing something? Have the preachers and teachers of the Word of God been doing damage to the cause of Christ?

"For my thoughts are not your thoughts, neither are your ways my ways, saith the Lord.
For as the heavens are higher than the earth, so are my ways higher than your ways, and my thoughts than your thoughts."

- Isaiah 55:8-9 (KJV)

What I have heard and read over the years from Christian authors and teachers of the Bible on the subject of being a successful Christian, more often than not refer to the following. Please note that this list is not exclusive:

1. Financial Prosperity – That is, to be successful, you must have a lot of money.
2. Assets – such as houses, cars, gold, bonds, etc.
3. Strategic Connections – You must be connected to the movers and shakers of lands.
4. Popularity – To be successful today, you must be popular in your community or constituency. For example, as a Minister of the Gospel, you must be a frequent speaker at the major conferences; you must be on TV, and in all the modern day medium of packaging. You must also be very high on the popularity ratings of the masses.
5. Education – No doubt education is one of the key factors that projects people as being successful. Can it be one of the reasons why so many people today are so keen on acquiring the honorary doctorate degree?
6. Size – By this, I mean the size of your business or church. Is it not true that most Christians will reckon ministers like Joel Osteen, T.D. Jakes, Pastor E.A. Adeboye, Bishop David Oyedepo, etc. as more successful than unknown ministers – like most ministers that we know or relate to?

Can we be making a grave mistake? Are we judging from man's outlook? Have we then not equated success in life and ministry to material prosperity? What then if I may ask makes us different from the world? May we be in for a surprise on the day of judgement?

Is it for no reason that God declares that what man celebrates, He disdains? Is it not to correct our erroneous judgement as God declares that His ways and thoughts are far higher than ours and that He does not see or judge from man's perspective?

Remember God's rebuke to the greatest prophets from Dan to Beersheba – Samuel, when he remarked:

> *"...for the Lord seeth not as man seeth; for man looketh on the outward appearance, but the LORD looketh on the heart."*
>
> - 1 Samuel 16:7b (KJV)

God's Definition of Success – FAITHFULNESS!

As I study the Bible, I realise that the highest form or level of success in the Kingdom of God is Faithfulness!

God, as it appears to me, is more concerned about my faithfulness than my material success. There seems to be such a craving for material success today that many of us are doing things that are spirituality injurious to our lives and the course of Christ.

In our pursuit of true success, we have totally gone the world's way. What seems to be of relevance to us in Christendom is ministerial packaging rather than faithfulness to God. How often as a Body of Christ, do we teach folks about being faithful to their calling and ministry? Most of the teachings we receive nowadays are centred on things of the flesh, covetousness and idolatry. We seem to have ignored what is critical and are rather chasing shadows such as money, titles, and toys. Sadly enough, this path has led us to the worship of Men of God! Many believers know more about their church leaders today than their Precious Saviour. A good number of pastors rather than being content with serving as "Men of God" have become "God of men".

Let's look at what Christ will be looking for when He returns – I will allow this scripture to speak for itself:

> *"His lord said unto him, Well done, thou good and faithful servant: thou hast been faithful over a few things, I will make thee ruler over many things: enter thou into the joy of thy lord."*
>
> - Matthew 25:21 (KJV)

The above passage is a picture of what to expect at the Judgement or BEMA seat. Christ commends His servants for their faithfulness. Again, in Luke 12:42-48, Jesus uses the Parable of the Faithful and Unfaithful Servants to illustrate the two possible ways of living open to all His followers in the light of His absence and promised return:

1. They can be faithful and obedient, ever watchful and spiritually ready for the Lord's return at any time, and they will receive their Master's blessing.

Or

2. They can grow careless and worldly minded, yearning that the Lord delays His coming, cease to resist sin and depart from the path of faithfulness; such as these will then receive God's condemnation and inherit everlasting shame and ruin at His coming.

The more I study the Bible, the more I realise that God's emphasis to Kingdom citizens is Faithfulness rather than Success! To qualify for true riches in the Kingdom of God, you must be faithful with unrighteous mammon!

> *"If therefore ye have not been faithful in the unrighteous mammon, who will commit to your trust the true riches?"*
>
> - Luke 16:11 (KJV)

How many of us are faithful with money? As God's servants, the fundamental requirements of our Master to us is Faithfulness; not Success! Moreover, it is required of stewards that they are found Faithful! The greatest commendation in the Kingdom seems to be Faithfulness.

> *"So then they which be of faith are blessed with faithful Abraham."*
>
> - Galatians 3:9 (KJV)

In the whole of the Old Testament corpus, I am not sure that there was a saint who surpassed Moses' outstanding service to God and Israel. How does the Bible describe him?

> *"Who was faithful to him that appointed him, as also Moses was faithful in all his house."*
>
> - Hebrews 3:2 (KJV)

> *"And Moses verily was faithful in all his house, as a servant, for a testimony of those things which were to be spoken after;"*
>
> - Hebrews 3:5 (KJV)

We are called to be faithful to God and our calling, not just when things are comfortable, but even in the face of death – this is the only way to receive the martyr's crown.

> *"Fear none of those things which thou shalt suffer: behold, the devil shall cast some of you into prison, that ye may be tried; and ye shall*

have tribulation ten days: be thou faithful unto death, and I will give thee a crown of life."

- Revelations 2:10 (KJV)

"I know thy works, and where thou dwellest, even where Satan's seat is: and thou holdest fast my name, and hast not denied my faith, even in those days wherein Antipas was my faithful martyr, who was slain among you, where Satan dwelleth."

- Revelations 2:13 (KJV)

I have repeatedly heard a lot of Pastors and church leaders complain about mediocrity in their ministries, church splits, and the lack of commitment, just to mention these few. It seems to me that what is lacking today is faithfulness.

"And the things that thou hast heard of me among many witnesses, the same commit thou to faithful men, who shall be able to teach others also."

- 2 Timothy 2:2 (KJV)

Did you notice the fundamental quality that spiritual leaders should be looking for among their protégées or would be disciples or leaders? – Faithfulness!

"By Silvanus, a faithful brother unto you, as I suppose…"

- 1 Peter 5:12a

From the foregoing, we can see that another word for success in God's Kingdom, particularly when it comes to service, is Faithfulness!

CHAPTER 13
WEAPONS OF MASS DISTRACTION

"All things are lawful unto me, but all things are not expedient: all things are lawful for me, but I will not be brought under the power of any."

- 1 Corinthians 6:12 (KJV)

"All things are lawful for me, but all things are not expedient: all things are lawful for me, but all things edify not."

- 1 Corinthians 10:23 (KJV)

Before the famous operation desert storm in 2003, the United States and Britain asserted that the late dictator, Saddam Hussein, possessed large, hidden stockpiles of weapons which they classified as being of mass destruction. The important thing, according to the reports, was that these weapons were capable of destroying the lives of thousands, if not millions. In the same vein, I believe Satan has released new weapons from his arsenal which are aimed at ensuring that Christians never focus on their God-given assignments, talk less of finishing it. This is what I call 'Weapons of Mass Distraction'!

Nothing aborts destinies and leads to a shipwreck of faith more than the power of distraction.

DISTRACTED DRIVING

According to reports from the United States of America (Top 25 Causes of Car Accidents), the number one reason for road accidents is distracted driving. The report states:

"The number one cause of car accidents is not criminals that drove drunk, sped or ran a red light. Distracted drivers are the top cause of car accidents in the US today. A distracted driver is a motorist that diverts his or her attention from the road, usually to talk on a cell phone, send a text message, or eat food." (Law office of Michael Pines, APC. 'Top 25 Causes of Accidents'. Serious Accidents, https://seriousaccidents. com/legal-advice/top-causes-of-car-accidents/. Accessed 26 October 2016.)

The same is true in the United Kingdom and many other countries. The number one cause of road accidents is distracted driving. How many destinies have been brought to an abrupt end because of distraction; how many today are wandering around in the wilderness of this world; how many people are not achieving much in life because they are distracted?

Unfortunately, most of the things that divide our attention from fulfilling our divine purpose or assignment are what you wouldn't call sins. They are not things that the Bible forbids. In fact, many of such things could come as a blessing. This is why Paul cautions believers from things that appear to be lawful, but may not be beneficial. These very things can be injurious to our spiritual health or divine assignment and can also be classified as weights – they slow us down or distract us from finishing our race.

> "Wherefore seeing we also are compassed about with so great a cloud of witnesses, let us lay aside every weight, and the sin which doth so easily beset us, and let us run with patience the race that is set before us"
>
> - Hebrews 12:1 (KJV)

SOME WEAPONS OF MASS DISTRACTION

I will like to identify a few weapons that Satan uses to distract us from focusing and ultimately completing our assignments in life. This list is in no way exhaustive. They include:

1. **People** – Many of whom are supposed 'friends' and even family members. They do more harm than good; they make you retrogress than

progress in pursuing and fulfilling your purpose.

2. **Job/Business** - It is stated in the Holy Word that he that does not work must not eat (2 Thessalonians 3:10). Work was created by God, and as individuals, we must endeavour to be hard-working and mind our own business (1 Thessalonians 4:11). However, there are many people who are engaged in certain jobs, professions or businesses that are more of a distraction than a blessing. These jobs, professions or businesses might have been a set up by the enemy to take them far from their God-given assignments.

3. **Pleasure** – No doubt this generation is filled with God-dishonouring and pleasure-seeking people. Paul, the apostle from Tarsus, prophesied that one of the key signs that will mark the days shortly before the second coming is that people will love pleasures more than they love God (2 Timothy 3:4).

   Someone may ask, "Is there anything wrong in seeking pleasure?" I don't think so. However, seeking it more than God or at the expense of fulfilling our divine assignment is wrong!

   Today, there are several ways that people seek pleasure, such that it becomes inimical or a distraction to their calling. When I was a young boy, I used to play and loved to watch football. Playing or watching football, in itself, may not be sinful but in this instance, it was so bad that quite regularly when a football match clashed with choir practice, I chose the former. There came a time when I had to make a choice. If anything takes the place of God or distracts us from fulfilling our higher calling, then we must call such leisure into question.

4. **Modern Technology** – Nothing has benefited and added value to our lives in the 20th and 21st centuries more than technology. Thanks to modern technology, many people are living longer and better. The world has also become a global village as knowledge has increased at a phenomenal rate.

Whilst celebrating these achievements, I personally believe that Satan's greatest weapon in distracting people from fulfilling their life's purpose and assignment is modern technology, to be specific – mobile phones.

Mobile phones have not only become the modern day golden calf but are also responsible for distracting people from carrying out and focusing on weightier matters. Most Christians today turn to their mobile phones more than they consult their Bibles. Do you know how many times the average person gets on their phone? It will shock you that many people spend more hours surfing the net; posting and reading things that have no bearing with their assignment in life, or godly living.

Have you noticed that social media has become an avenue to display our heighted desire for things of the flesh? Many of us who are Ministers of the Gospel are simply engaged in self-promotion. Satan is strategically using technology to distract and destroy many destinies.

I pray that God will deliver us from these weapons of mass distraction, in order for us to be able to focus on our assignments!

CHAPTER 14

KEYS TO COMPLETING YOUR ASSIGNMENT

I have often declared that 'when you see the glory, ask for the story'. Behind every glory, major achievement, invention and breakthrough, there are untold stories. Nothing ever happens in isolation. For every prize, there's a press!

In this chapter, I will like to highlight a few important keys or components, necessary for completing our life's assignment:

1. **Hard work** – No lazy person ever achieves much in life. To complete your God-given assignment, you must be a hard worker. Jesus worked tirelessly throughout His short stay on earth. Paul declared that he laboured more abundantly than other apostles or his contemporaries. Ask

the Olympic runners, no one ever won a gold medal without working hard.

2. **Sacrifice** – To finish your race and complete your assignment, you will have to sacrifice or give up a number of things. They may be certain pleasures, relationships, achievements, ambitions, dreams, and even worldly possessions.

3. **Determination** – You must possess the dogged ruggedness of a bulldog. You must be a person that will not give up easily. In the face of all forms of adversity, tragedy or setback, you must be determined to complete your race or assignment.

4. **Taking Initiative** – Most people never accomplish much in life because they are always waiting for the right timing, atmosphere, personnel etc. Rather than always waiting for things to happen, you must be a person that makes things happen if you will finish your assignment.

5. **Team player** – Whatever we have been called to do in this life, we can never do in isolation. You must learn to work in a team! No man is an island. Someone else always has something that you need. Jesus needed a team in order to finish his assignment; so also did Paul. There's multiplied power when we team up with other strategic partners. It might take humility to ask others for help.

One who is granted many keys to open great doors is sure to achieve mighty feats as compared to one who is ignorant. Having journeyed with me throughout this book, it is my firm belief that your mind has not only be renewed but that your heart has been gripped with a burning desire to identify your call and finish your race. May God grant us all grace!

SPECIAL INVITATION

I am totally convinced that this book did not come into your hands by sheer accident – it was orchestrated by God!

If you have never at any point in time opened up your heart to receive Jesus and accept Him as your Lord and Personal Saviour – you can do so right now!

Why not say this short prayer?

Dear Jesus! Thank you for dying on the Cross for me. I believe you died and God raised you up on the third day for my salvation. I accept you today as my Lord and Personal Saviour.
Thank you for saving me! Amen!

OTHER TITLES FROM THE SAME AUTHOR

If this book has touched you, why not place an order for other books!

CONTACT DETAILS

World Harvest Christian Centre
Great Commission House
25-27 Ruby Street
off Old Kent Road
London SE15 1LL
Tel: + 44 (020) 7358 8080

World Harvest Christian Centre
Enmore Road
South Norwood
London SE25 5NQ
Tel: + 44 (020) 86545649

Email: admin@worldharvest.org.uk
website: www.worldharvest.org.uk
Facebook: World Harvest Christian Centre, London
Twitter: @whcc_london, @PastorWale_